war

THE WORLD REACTS

Paul Bennett

 Belitha Press

FOREWORD

Disasters affect everyone. At some point in your life, you have a good chance of being caught in one or of knowing somebody who is caught in one.

For most of us, the disaster may be a car crash or a house fire, and the police, fire or ambulance service will be on hand to help. But for millions of people around the world, disasters happen far more often and are more catastrophic.

Some countries suffer frequent natural disasters, such as floods, earthquakes and droughts. They do not always have the resources to deal with the crisis and it is usually the poorest people who are the most affected and least able to recover.

War is a humanmade disaster that ruins people's lives. The effects of droughts and floods are made worse when there is war.

When people find they are unable to cope with a disaster, they need the help of aid agencies, such as the Red Cross.

Aid agencies react quickly to emergencies, bringing help to those in need. Usually it is when this international aid begins to flow that you hear about a disaster in the news.

The World Reacts series ties in closely with the work of the International Federation of Red Cross and Red Crescent Societies. The Federation coordinates international disaster relief and promotes development around the world, to prevent and alleviate human suffering. There is a Red Cross or Red Crescent society in almost every country of the world. Last year we helped 22 million people caught up in disaster.

This series will help you to understand the problems faced by people threatened by disaster and to see how you can help. We hope that you enjoy these books.

George Weber
Secretary General, International Federation
of Red Cross and Red Crescent Societies

◄ *The Red Cross symbol (left) was first created to protect the wounded in war and those who cared for them. The Red Crescent symbol (right) is used by Muslim countries around the world. Both symbols have equal status.*

CONTENTS

Words in **bold** appear in the glossary on page 31.

WHAT IS WAR?

War is a violent argument between countries. It can also be between different sides within a country. This is called civil war.

Why do wars happen?

We often see pictures of soldiers fighting on the television news. But why do soldiers try to kill or injure each other?

Wars happen for many reasons. They may start because a country wants more land and power, and so **invades** another country. They may be fought over resources – over good farmland or land that is rich in minerals, such as oil or gold.

Wars also start because of differences of religion or because one group in a country wants to gain power over another group.

Wars in history

There have been wars throughout history. There were two world wars this century – the First World War (1914–18) and the Second World War (1939–45) – which involved many different countries.

Most of today's wars are civil wars fought between groups within a country. Many of these wars have happened in the world's poorest countries.

◄ *A Cambodian girl carries a rifle. Girls are sometimes forced to fight in armed conflicts.*

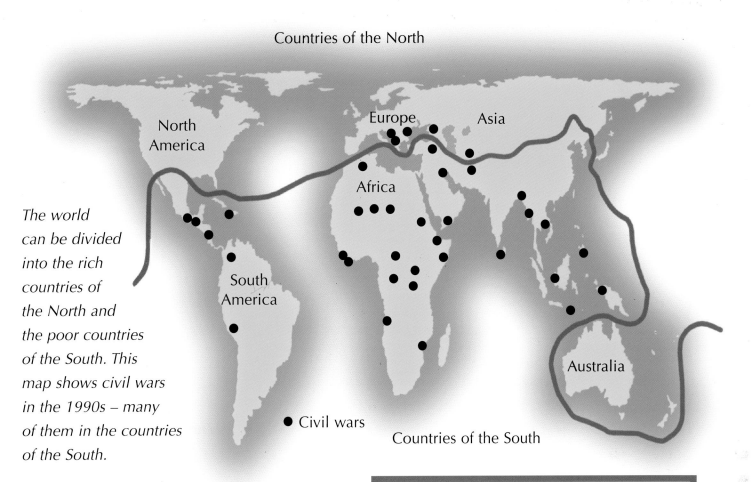

The world can be divided into the rich countries of the North and the poor countries of the South. This map shows civil wars in the 1990s – many of them in the countries of the South.

● Civil wars

Countries of the South

A new age of peace?

At the end of the 1980s, many people hoped there would be a new age of peace because the Cold War had ended. This was the period after the Second World War when the USA, with its western **allies**, and the former **Soviet Union**, with its eastern allies, built up powerful armed forces and threatened to attack each other.

But the 1990s have not been a new age of peace. In fact, the number of wars has increased. These wars have been mostly civil wars in poor countries, with battles fought across fields and villages.

Ordinary people suffer most when there is war. Nine out of ten people killed in war are not soldiers but innocent **civilians** and most of them are women and children.

The world maps used in this book are Peters' projection maps. Peters' projection – named after Arno Peters who made the map – is an accurate way of seeing the world, because it shows the actual size of countries.

Aid in action

War: The World Reacts looks at what happens when there is war and how the world can help. It takes examples of wars around the world and looks at the help given by governments and **aid agencies**.

This book aims to help you understand why wars happen and how ordinary people are affected. It will help you see what can be done to help the victims of war and how important peace is for everyone.

PEOPLE ON THE MOVE

When war breaks out, people leave their homes to escape the fighting. This means thousands of people may be on the move.

Travelling in safety

People leave their villages for the safety of towns and cities or they cross the border into another country.

They may be driven from their homes by **ethnic** cleansing, which is sometimes one of the aims of civil war. This is when one group of people tries to force all other ethnic groups out of an area. Ethnic cleansing has led to the killing of whole communities.

Governments and aid agencies try to make sure that people escaping conflict can travel in safety. This may be difficult as some countries do not want outside forces interfering with their problems and will not let them in. Aid agencies may find it impossible to help people. Often people only find protection once they cross a border and enter another country.

▼ *Refugees from Zaire travel by boat across Lake Tanganyika to find safety in neighbouring Tanzania.*

Who is a refugee?

Refugees are people who have been forced to leave their country – often because they fear for their lives. They give up their homes, jobs and families to find safety.

The office of the **United Nations** High Commissioner for Refugees (UNHCR) began its work in 1951. It was set up to help people who had fled their country. Now it also helps internally displaced people – people who have fled because of war or fear of **persecution** but have not crossed the border into another country.

Yugoslavia 1991–92
Fleeing the fighting

Yugoslavia was a popular place in Europe for people to go on holiday. Then in 1991–92, the country split apart when some of the **republics** that made up Yugoslavia, including Croatia, Slovenia, Bosnia and Macedonia, announced that they were now **independent** countries. Fighting broke out almost immediately between groups over land.

Millions on the move

During the next five years, four million people were forced to leave their homes – the biggest movement of people in Europe since the Second World War. Thousands were killed because of ethnic cleansing.

▲ *War disrupts everyday life. In many cities in the former Yugoslavia, children couldn't travel to school, because of the danger of being shot at.*

Amra, a 13-year-old Bosnian refugee, remembers how she became separated from her sister, Elma, during the war:

'The war broke out and I saw many people killed... My mother told us we should go to Croatia. She tried to fetch Elma, but there was an explosion and she couldn't reach her... We lived in a refugee centre in Croatia for two months. One day some people came and asked us if we wanted to go to Switzerland. So we left Croatia.'

This Bosnian child was forced to leave his home because of fighting.

SAFETY FOR CIVILIANS

When there is war, innocent people need protection. The United Nations (UN) tries to protect civilians by setting up safe areas in war zones.

Safe havens

Safe havens are places in a war zone that are free from fighting. People go to these areas to find safety and to get help from aid agencies who provide them with food, water, medicine and shelter.

Safe areas are a good idea, but they do not always work. They are rarely set up with the agreement of all sides in a war, and soldiers are sometimes allowed into these areas. This means that they are often a target for attack by warring groups, making them far from safe. With this threat of attack, aid agencies may find it difficult to help civilians in a safe zone.

▼ *UN troops guard a safe haven for Kurdish refugees near the Turkish–Iraqi border. The Kurds fled because they feared Iraqi attacks.*

Staying neutral

It is important that aid agencies remain neutral – that they do not favour one warring group over another. The International Committee of the Red Cross (ICRC) has a special role to help the victims of war – civilians, wounded soldiers and **prisoners of war** – on both sides of a conflict. Other aid agencies are also neutral. They know that the success of their work depends on not taking sides. But not everyone accepts the neutrality of aid agencies and often they are not allowed into a country. This means that they cannot always reach the victims of war.

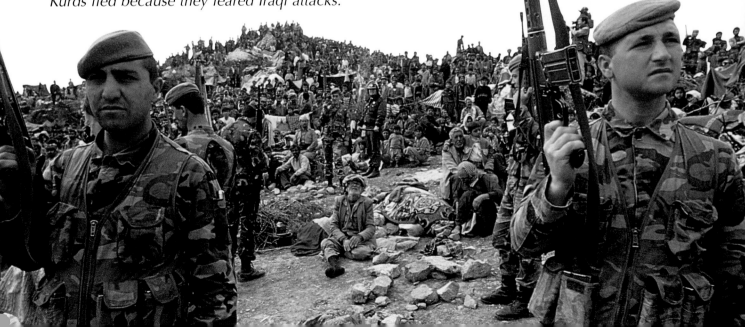

Rwanda 1994

Helping both sides

When civil war broke out in Rwanda in 1994, it was difficult for aid agencies to protect civilians and to appear neutral.

Conflict between the Hutu and Tutsi groups in the country began in April 1994 when the Hutu president of Rwanda was killed and Hutus blamed Tutsis for the killing. More than half a million Tutsis were then killed by the Hutus.

Hutu leaders were forced to leave Rwanda. In a matter of days, over two million Hutus followed them and crossed the borders into the neighbouring countries of Zaire, Tanzania and Burundi.

▲ *A Rwandan family loads belongings into a truck and flees the country.*

▲ *A Rwandan boy, separated from his family during civil war, is protected by a United Nations soldier.*

Caught in the crossfire

Aid agencies were caught between the rival groups, but they had to help the Hutu refugees, some of whom had killed Tutsis.

The United Nations set up safe areas in Rwanda. Over one million people, mainly Hutus, found protection in a safe zone in the southwest of the country.

As the months passed, the Tutsi-led government became impatient for people to return home. It saw the camps, mainly inhabited by Hutus, as a threat. So in April 1995, the government started moving people home. People in the camps were threatened with guns and about 3000 were killed. Some say that this was **revenge** for the **massacre** of Tutsis that had taken place a year earlier.

AID IN A WAR ZONE

Bringing emergency aid to people in a war zone is a huge job and can be very dangerous.

Organizing relief

Aid agencies need permission from warring sides to give **aid** in a war zone. Even when this permission is given, aid workers are often stopped and threatened by soldiers. There is also the danger that aid agency vehicles, radios, food and medical supplies will be stolen by an army for its own use.

The delivery of aid needs lots of organization and cooperation between the groups involved. Aid agencies must work together to prevent delays and so avoid unnecessary suffering. Sometimes aid agencies divide up the tasks between them. For example, one agency looks after the water supplies, another looks after toilets and medical care and another is responsible for providing food.

▲ *A young Iraqi boy balances a pot of fresh water sachets sent by the Red Cross during the* **Gulf War**.

Aid under fire

Bringing aid to a war zone can be very dangerous. Aid workers are often caught up in the middle of the fighting, so they sometimes wear bullet-proof vests and helmets to protect themselves (left). Violence may be used against them, if they are seen as taking sides in a conflict or they may be taken **hostage** by one of the warring groups. Some Red Cross workers, for example, have been murdered. This has caused aid agencies to think very hard about their role in times of conflict.

Somalia 1994

Fighting clans

The civil war in Somalia began in 1988. A large part of the population was forced to cross the border into neighbouring countries, where relief camps were set up. Farmers could no longer tend their crops because of the conflict, and **drought** and war at the same time caused food shortages and famine.

Controlling aid

Aid agencies had difficulties delivering aid to Somalians because of the number of tribal groups, or clans, fighting each another. Everything had to be done through local warlords, who controlled law and order. Even in relief camps, food supplies were controlled by clan leaders. Aid workers were accused of favouring one clan over another and fighting often broke out in the camps.

▲ *This Somalian soldier waits for a delivery of food aid by truck. Warlords made the delivery of aid almost impossible.*

Overcoming the obstacles

Despite all these difficulties, aid agencies have continued to help the people of Somalia. **Médecins Sans Frontières (MSF)**, for example, opened a clinic in the Bakool area of the country. Local people wanted help that wouldn't attract the warlords' attention. Twelve Somali aid workers and an MSF nurse now work at the centre.

◄ *Food aid was looted or stolen by warlords to feed their armies as soon as it arrived at a port.*

APPEALS FOR AID

Aid supplies run short as more and more people arrive at relief camps. Soon more help is needed.

Emergency response

Aid agencies send in emergency response teams to assess the needs of people in relief camps. Some of the refugees may have walked for days to reach a camp and are weak when they arrive. Others may have bullet or bomb wounds which need urgent treatment.

People need emergency food and water. They also need tents for shelter, as well as blankets and clothes to keep them warm.

Aid agencies work hard to give out food supplies and to care for the sick and wounded. They dig toilets and drill wells for water. People need clean and safe water as quickly as possible, because dirty water can spread disease.

Some aid agencies keep stores of aid supplies ready to ship to a country when there is an emergency. Sometimes the United Nations makes appeals to governments around the world for their help.

War and famine

War is one of the main causes of famine. It forces farmers to abandon their crops and animals. Whole harvests are left to rot, as people leave their homes to escape the fighting.

When the rains do not come, harvests fail and people go hungry. When there is drought and war at the same time, the result is nearly always famine.

During a food shortage, prices rise and people have to pay more for less food. People fleeing conflict often cannot afford to buy any food. Without help from aid agencies, they may starve.

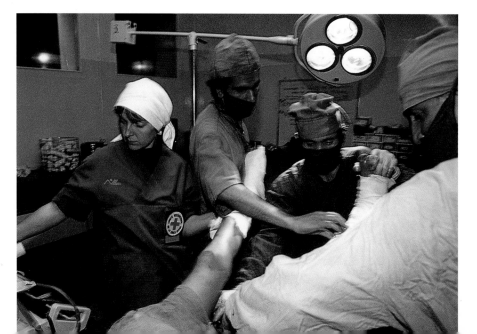

◀ Red Cross doctors and nurses are sent in to war zones to save lives. Here they are treating an injured person in a hospital in Kabul, the war-torn capital of Afghanistan.

Chechnya 1994

Flash appeal

After the end of the Cold War, many republics of the former Soviet Union wanted to rule themselves. Chechnya was one of the republics that wanted independence, and this led to fighting with the government of Russia.

▲ *Russian troops patrol the ruins of Grozny, Chechnya's capital city.*

Crossing borders

In December 1994, Russian government forces crossed the border into Chechnya. Many people died in the fighting that followed and hundreds of thousands fled into neighbouring republics.

An appeal for help

The Russian government asked for help to cope with this mass movement of people. In January 1995, the United Nations High Commissioner for Refugees sent workers to Chechnya to assess the emergency. A month later, there was a flash appeal to countries around the world for donations.

Help at hand

The money raised was spent on shelter, toilets, and stoves and pots for cooking. Some of the money was also spent on improving transport and health care.

The war in Chechnya ended in August 1996, and in 1997 there were **elections** to vote for a new independent government.

▶ *Children in Grozny play in front of their bombed-out school.*

RELIEF CONVOYS

Convoys of trucks may have to travel long distances to deliver aid to a war zone. Their journey is sometimes made difficult by road blocks and the threat of attack.

Moving supplies

Delivering relief supplies to a war zone is a difficult job. Ports, roads and railways may be damaged and supplies have to be flown to more remote areas.

Most aid is sent by ship and delivered to ports. But if a country is not on the coast, supplies have to travel through neighbouring countries. Railways are the best way of moving supplies overland, because thousands of tonnes can be moved on a single journey. But trains only run on certain routes and cannot deliver to every village.

Convoys of trucks are often used to transport aid, because they can travel almost anywhere by road.

Red Cross food parcels

The Red Cross is famous for the food parcels it distributes in emergencies around the world. What goes into a parcel depends on the country it is going to, because the contents have to suit the people's diet. For example, in Georgia, one of the former Soviet republics, the parcels were made up of: 6 kg wheatflour; 3 kg rice; 2 kg sugar; 2 kg kidney beans; 2 kg pasta; 2 litres vegetable oil; 100g yeast; 600g tinned beef; 600g soap; and candles and matches. Each parcel fed one person for two months. The parcels were put together by local people and given to those most in need.

▼ *The United Nations protects a convoy of trucks delivering aid to a war zone.*

Sudan 1991
Shipping the aid

There has been civil war in Sudan since 1983. Many people have been displaced and killed, and food supplies have also been hit. Years of drought in the early 1990s combined with war to bring famine to Sudan.

A ship's journey
The Dutch Red Cross sent food supplies to the victims of war and famine in 1991. Its ship, the *Darfur*, left Rotterdam in Holland on 2 May and headed down the coast of France, around Spain and into the Mediterranean Sea. She then sailed through the Suez Canal and through the Red Sea, arriving in Port Sudan on 2 June.

▲ *Food aid is unloaded at Port Sudan. The 4000 km journey from northern Europe took one month.*

▼ *From the ship, sacks of grain are loaded on to trucks.*

Moving the aid
The *Darfur* docked and was unloaded as quickly as possible. Supplies were then moved by rail or road. Eight thousand tonnes of aid went by rail to Khartoum – the capital of Sudan – each month, and truck convoys took more there by road.

From Khartoum, food supplies were driven to distribution centres in the south of the country. People came to these centres to collect the food.

KEEPING THE PEACE

Only peace can bring people hope for the future. The United Nations (UN) plays an important role in bringing peace to war-torn countries.

The United Nations

Since the end of the Cold War, the world has turned more and more to the United Nations to deal with conflicts. The UN encourages warring sides to stop fighting and to build a peaceful future together.

The Security Council is the part of the UN responsible for peacekeeping. With the agreement of warring sides, it oversees peace agreements and **cease-fires** and tries to stop disagreements between groups before they turn into full-scale war. The Council also has the power to bring **sanctions** or penalties against warring countries.

UN troops or soldiers, with their blue helmets, are often used for peacekeeping. They carry arms, but they can only use them in special circumstances to defend themselves. The UN also works to make sure that elections are carried out fairly and without violence.

▼ *The UN monitored Cambodian elections in 1993 to make sure they were carried out fairly.*

Human rights

Treaties are agreements by different countries to obey the same law. Some treaties protect **human rights**. These include laws against **racism**, cruel treatment or punishment of people, and the rights of children.

In a war zone, these laws are often ignored. Part of the work of the United Nations is to act against people who break these laws and to restore human rights.

For example, in the former Yugoslavia, the United Nations continues to watch over certain areas to make sure that human rights are protected.

Iraq 1991
Protecting the Kurds

Kurdish people have lived in Iraq for thousands of years, but have not been allowed to keep their own language and culture there.

After the Gulf War of 1990–91, there was a Kurdish **uprising** against the Iraqi government. It was unsuccessful, and about one and a half million Kurds left their homes for the Turkish–Iraqi border because they feared Iraqi attacks.

Kurdish human rights

The United Nations decided to set up a safe area without agreement from the Iraqi government. This is because Iraq had ignored Kurdish human rights in the past. It had used **chemical weapons** against the Kurds in 1988, killing many women and children. The UN also brought economic sanctions – restrictions on trade with other countries – against Iraq at the beginning of the Gulf War when Iraq invaded Kuwait.

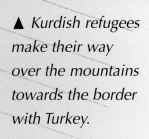

▲ *Kurdish refugees make their way over the mountains towards the border with Turkey.*

Iraq **blockaded** the safe haven, and prevented aid agencies from entering because it disagreed with the UN's actions. Aid agencies tried to distance themselves from the UN, hoping that Iraq would let them do their work. But this didn't happen and they had to bring in supplies without Iraqi permission.

◄ *Aid agencies deliver water to Kurdish refugees in the UN safe zone.*

REUNITING FAMILIES

Many of the refugees in a war zone are children on their own. They get split up from their families and may end up far away from home.

Tracing programmes

Once the fighting is over, children need to be reunited with their families as soon as possible. Aid agencies, such as the Red Cross, run tracing programmes to help children find their relatives.

They begin their work by registering the children and finding out what happened to them. Once they know a child's name and the area she came from, they can start trying to trace her parents or relatives – by using photos and radio messages and by visiting her home area.

This is not easy. Family members may have fled their homes or they may have been killed in the fighting. Sometimes parents or relatives cannot be traced and substitute parents are found to look after a child until she is grown up and can look after herself.

◀ *This Rwandan girl holds up her registration number for the photographer. The photo will be used to try to trace her family.*

Basic rights

An international agreement, called the Convention on the Rights of the Child, gives everyone under 18 the right to safety, shelter, food, water, health and education. Many countries have signed this treaty, but still children lack these rights. Many children experience war at first hand – like the Bosnian child who drew the picture above.

When they become refugees in another country, children lose the protection of their government. Many lose the protection of their families too. This is why the Convention covers the rights of refugee children: if you are a refugee you have the right to special protection.

Afghanistan 1995

Searching for an uncle

There has been civil war in Afghanistan since 1988. During an attack on the capital city of Kabul in 1995, a ten-year-old boy called Ghulam Nabi escaped unhurt when his house was flattened by a shell. But his father and brother were both killed in the attack.

In the confusion that followed, Ghulam fled to Kandahar, where he ended up in a school. He couldn't remember anything about his journey or how he got there.

He wanted to return to Kabul and join his only living relative, his uncle, so he went to the **Red Crescent** for help.

Ten-year-old Ghulam was reunited with his uncle by the Red Crescent.

The tracing trail

The Afghan Red Crescent took all Ghulam's details – his name, his age and his uncle's name and address. They also took details of where his uncle worked in case his uncle's home had been destroyed.

This information was sent to the Red Crescent in Kabul, and a case worker there traced Ghulam's uncle. The uncle was told what had happened to his nephew and that Ghulam wanted to come and live with him. When he said he would care for Ghulam, the Red Crescent flew Ghulam to Kabul where he was reunited with his uncle.

◄ Tanks in the war-torn capital of Kabul.

RETURNING HOME

When the war is over, refugees are encouraged to return home as soon as possible. But before they return home, they must know they can travel safely.

After the fighting

The journey home may be a long one by foot, so returnees – people returning home – are given supplies for their journey. Aid agencies set up way stations, where people receive food, water and medical help on the way home.

Sometimes refugees are allowed to stay in the country they have fled to. Aid agencies may help them build new lives there, but only with the government's permission. Often permission is not given, because the country is poor and cannot cope with thousands of refugees.

Refugees may also go to another country that is willing to take them for a short time on the condition that they are resettled elsewhere in the future.

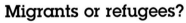

▶ *A Rwandan woman and her son return home after five months in a refugee camp in Zaire.*

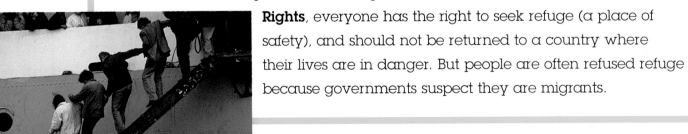

Migrants or refugees?

Migrants are people who leave their country to seek a better life and more money in another country. Unlike refugees, they do not fear for their lives and may return home whenever they wish. According to the **Universal Declaration of Human Rights**, everyone has the right to seek refuge (a place of safety), and should not be returned to a country where their lives are in danger. But people are often refused refuge because governments suspect they are migrants.

Myanmar 1997

Going home

Over the past three years, 250 000 refugees have left Bangladesh to return home to Myanmar (formerly known as Burma) in the largest **repatriation** ever organized in Asia.

The Rohingya people are a **minority group** in Myanmar. They first entered Bangladesh in 1991–92 to escape persecution in their country. Some crossed the mountains into Bangladesh by foot or on bicycles. Others travelled there by boat.

Bangladesh is one of the world's poorest countries and had very few resources to look after the refugees. But with the help of aid agencies, around 20 camps were set up throughout the country to provide homes for tens of thousands of Rohingyas.

▲ *A UNHCR worker (centre) accompanies a widow and her children returning to Myanmar.*

▲ *Returnee women weaving baskets from cane bamboo.*

Leaving Bangladesh

The Myanmar government agreed to take the Rohingyas back in 1997. The United Nations High Commissioner for Refugees (UNHCR) went with them, to make sure that they had a safe journey back.

The UNHCR also helped people once they had arrived home. Many of the returnees had never learned to write their own language before they fled to Bangladesh, so UNHCR helped to fund projects to teach them. It also set up projects to repair schools and hospitals, and gave small loans to people to restart their own businesses in some of the traditional crafts of pot-making and basket-weaving.

REBUILDING LIVES

Returnees are given advice and help to rebuild their lives. Those who are resettled need support to help them adapt to a new life in a new country.

A new start

Returnees are given help to start again. They are given everyday items, such as cooking pots, salt and soap. Farmers are given tools and seed so that they can start to grow their own food again. People who live near lakes or rivers are given fishing nets, so that they can provide extra food for their families.

Training is also given so that people can help themselves. This includes training in raising farm animals, **irrigation** and ways to control crop-eating **pests.**

Refugees who have been resettled in another country may find it difficult to make a new start. Often they do not know the language

▲ *Education is important to help children lead a normal life again.*

and customs of the country. Without help to learn the language and to adapt to the way of life, it may be difficult for them to settle in their new home.

Child soldiers

The Convention on the Rights of the Child says that if you are under 15, you should never take part in war. But across the world there are soldiers as young as six fighting on the front line. Child soldiers (left) may have been kidnapped and forced to fight. They may have lost their parents in war and so the army becomes their 'family', providing food, clothing and shelter. Whatever the reasons, the effects on children of fighting in a war are very damaging. Those who survive may suffer nightmares, or become aggressive and withdrawn.

Cambodia 1993

Starting again

For over 25 years, the people of Cambodia have had very little peace. Civil war, changes in government and invasion by other countries have caused the deaths of millions of people and many hundreds of thousands have fled the country.

More than 240 000 people went to live in refugee camps in Thailand. Between 1992 and 1993, all these refugees returned to Cambodia with the help of the United Nations. Some were given tools and a plot of farmland. Others were given food and small loans to start again.

But many of the refugees who had hoped to return as farmers have been unable to farm the land. This is because much of the Cambodian countryside is littered with **land mines**.

▲ *These Cambodian children, born in Thailand, see their country for the first time from a train window.*

Many Cambodian children were born in Thai camps and have never seen their own country. Others, like 13-year-old Narin, spent most of their lives in refugee camps in Thailand:

'For most of my life, my home was Site 2, a big refugee camp in Thailand. But Site 2 was not that bad. I studied very hard, because education leads to a good job. My mother and father left us, and so now I live in an orphanage. I wish I could have my family back.'

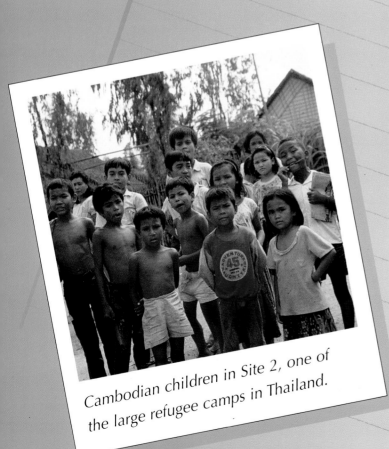

Cambodian children in Site 2, one of the large refugee camps in Thailand.

DANGEROUS MINES

Land mines are explosives that are placed in the ground in war zones. They are set off by stepping on them and they kill and injure innocent people.

People at risk

Land mines are laid in the ground by hand or scattered from the air during wartime. They are supposed to be a weapon against soldiers, but they threaten innocent people long after the fighting has finished.

Children are particularly at risk from mines. They run around and play on land that has been mined. They are small, so their bodies are close to the blast. This means that their injuries are often worse than those of adults.

There are about 119 million unexploded mines in 71 countries world wide. The worst affected countries are Cambodia, Angola, Afghanistan and the former Yugoslavia.

Clearing mines is a huge job. Trained people risk their lives to dig them out and make them safe. Many governments support mine clearance, but two million new mines are laid each year in war zones around the world, so clearing them is a huge task.

◄ *Digging out a land mine is slow and dangerous work.*

Banning land mines

The only solution to the problem of land mines is to ban them, so that no one makes or uses them. A ban on land mines has at last become a possibility. An international treaty to ban them was signed in December 1997 by over 120 countries. The countries that signed the treaty now hope that every country in the world will eventually sign.

Angola 1997

Living with land mines

After 20 years of civil war in Angola, peace has now given people a chance to rebuild their lives. But there are nine million land mines scattered across the country – one mine for each person – and this is a major problem that people will face for years to come.

More than 70 000 Angolans have lost their limbs through land mine explosions, and at least the same number have died. Two-thirds of the victims are between 16 and 30 years old.

Land mines have a devastating effect on people's lives. Injured people are unable to work and find it difficult to support themselves and their families. Mines also prevent good land from being farmed.

► *An Angolan girl learns to walk again using her false leg.*

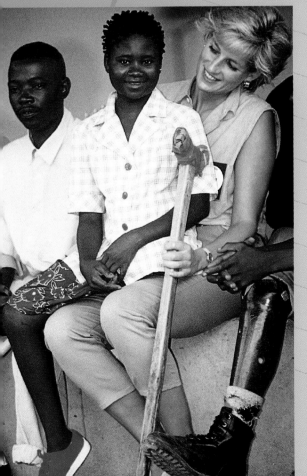

◄ *Diana, Princess of Wales, visits land mine victims in Angola in 1997.*

Helping land mine victims

Aid agencies provide medical help and equipment for land mine victims in Angola and other countries around the world. They run workshops which make false limbs and centres where victims are fitted with the limbs and taught how to walk again.

The late Diana, Princess of Wales, visited Red Cross workshops in Angola in January 1997, eight months before her death. Her visit helped to attract attention from all over the world to the suffering caused by land mines.

NEW CHALLENGES

The wars that have broken out since the end of the Cold War have led to new challenges for aid agencies. Aid agencies are looking closely at the way they help in an emergency.

Complicated crises

Today's emergencies are very complicated. They often include civil war, ethnic conflict, the mass movement of people, changes in governments, disputes over borders and, in many cases, drought and famine.

Aid organizations have had to look at better ways of dealing with these crises. All those involved in disaster relief – governments, aid agencies and international organizations – now work together to help in an emergency. A **Code of Conduct** has been created for everyone to follow when responding to a disaster. But for the Code to work the country receiving help must respect the work of the agencies. Otherwise they may be seen as taking sides, and this will prevent them helping people caught up in disaster.

▲ *During war, soldiers take food that is meant for ordinary people.*

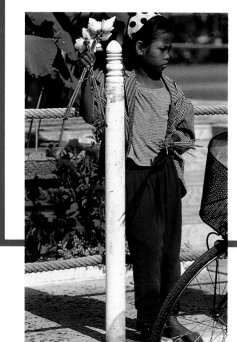

Relief and development

Poverty is one of the main causes of civil war in many countries of the South. Poor living conditions, lack of food and water, and the feeling of being powerless all create tension and unrest.

For these reasons, development – long-term ways of increasing people's standard of living – is important both for the prevention of conflict and for long-term peace.

Mozambique 1990s

Looking to the future

There was civil war in Mozambique for 17 years. During this time, nearly two million refugees fled to other countries and a further four million were displaced within the country. In 1992, a peace agreement was signed to bring an end to the fighting and in 1994, elections were held in Mozambique, supervised by a United Nations peacekeeping force.

◄ *Children play in front of a wall painted with scenes of guns and fighting.*

Aid for Mozambique

During the first years of peace, help was given by aid agencies to restore health care, water supplies and education. Farmers were given seed to grow crops and over seven million farm tools were distributed. Roads were repaired and new ones built, and land mines were cleared.

There are many ways for Mozambique to develop its **economy**. It has rich mineral resources for mining and good beaches for tourism.

As long as there is peace, Mozambique will need less help from outside and will eventually become **self-sufficient**.

▼ *One of Mozambique's beaches. Tourism could be a good source of income for the country.*

WORKING FOR PEACE

Poor people are made poorer by the effects of war.
Aid agencies give emergency help in war zones
and work to prevent conflicts in the future.

Preventing conflict

In many countries, there has been little improvement
in the lives of the poorest people. People continue
to suffer from bad health, because of lack of food
and clean drinking water, and still live in poor
housing. As we have seen, the unhappiness that poverty
brings means a greater risk of conflict in these countries.

Aid agencies help to improve people's lives by
supporting long-term projects. These projects help local
people to grow food, improve water supplies and earn
a living. This long-term aid work gives people more
independence and helps them to build for the future.

Aid agencies are working to bring an end to the
arms trade in which millions of cheap weapons are
sold to the poorer nations of the world. They also
encourage countries to trade only with nations that
support peace. These are all ways of preventing
conflict in the future.

The Red Cross

The Red Cross is the world's
largest organization which
cares for people in peace
and war. There are national
Red Cross and Red Crescent
Societies in almost every
country of the world, caring
for people at home and
abroad. The International
Committee of the Red Cross
(ICRC) helps the victims of
war, during and after the
fighting. The International
Federation of Red Cross and
Red Crescent Societies helps
refugees and people caught
up in natural disasters.

◀ *A United Nations soldier at a
checkpoint in war-torn Somalia.*

Tajikistan 1993
Heading for home

Civil war broke out in Tajikistan in late 1992, soon after it became independent from the former Soviet Union. The fighting was mainly in the southwest of the country and by January 1993 the conflict had ended.

Although the civil war did not last long, the fighting was very brutal and forced more than one million people – one-fifth of the population – to leave their homes. More than 65 000 Tajiks crossed the border into neighbouring Afghanistan because they feared being killed.

▲ *A widow and her children stand in front of the ruins that were once their home.*

An end to the conflict

When the war ended, people began to return to their villages, but many found that their belongings had been stolen or their homes had been burned down. The United Nations High Commissioner for Refugees (UNHCR) helped refugees in Afghanistan to cross the border back into Tajikistan and provided building materials to rebuild homes destroyed by the civil war. By 1997, most of the people had returned home.

▲ *After the fighting, farmers returned to their fields to start growing crops again.*

HOW YOU CAN HELP

War destroys people's lives.
Only peace can bring people
hope for the future.

● Make a display for your school showing aspects of the world's refugee problem. Find out where the main refugee populations are and mark them on a world map.

● Find out about aid agencies you would like to help (see addresses below). Organize a fundraising activity, such as a sponsored swim or run. Design your own sponsorship form and give information about how the money will be spent. Donate the money to the aid agency of your choice.

● Collect newspaper reports about wars around the world. What reasons are given for these conflicts?

● Write a letter to your local politician, asking him or her to support refugees. Some aid agencies, such as the UNHCR, rely on governments to donate money for their work.

● Contact a refugee family in your area (your local council could help you). Invite them to come and talk to your class. Your friendship could make them feel more welcome in their new country and will help you to understand the problems they face.

Finding out more

Visit the web sites of these organizations. Find out about their work and see how you can help.

British Red Cross
9 Grosvenor Crescent
London SW1X 7EJ
Telephone: 0171 235 5454
http://www.redcross.org.uk

OXFAM
274 Banbury Road
Oxford OX2 7DZ
Telephone: 01865 313600
http://www.oxfam.org.uk

Save the Children Fund (SCF)
17 Grove Lane
London SE5 8RD
Telephone: 0171 703 5400
http://www.oneworld.org/scf/

Amnesty International UK (information on human rights)
99–119 Rosebery Avenue
London EC1R 4RE
Telephone: 0171 814 6200
http://www.amnesty.org.uk/

Refugee Council (information on refugee issues)
3 Bondway
London SW8 1SJ
Tel: 0171 820 3000
http://www.gn.apc.org/refugeecounciluk

United Nations High Commissioner for Refugees (UNHCR)
Millbank Tower
21–24 Millbank
London SW1P 4QP
Telephone: 0171 828 9191
http://www.unhcr.ch

The International Committee of the Red Cross
Public Information Division
19 avenue de la Paix
CH 1202
Geneva
Switzerland
Telephone: 00 41 22 734 6001
http://www.icrc.org

The International Federation of Red Cross and Red Crescent Societies
17 chemin des Crêts
Petit-Saconnex
PO Box 372
CH-1211
Geneva 19
Switzerland
Telephone: 00 41 22 730 4222
http://www.ifrc.org

GLOSSARY

aid Resources given by one country, or organization, to another country. Aid is given to help people in an emergency and to improve their lives in the longer term.

aid agency An organization that helps people when there is a disaster and runs long-term projects to help people in poorer countries.

ally A country that is allied with another country through a treaty or agreement. Allied countries often fight on the same side in a war.

blockade To block off an area, so that no vehicles or people can get through.

cease-fire An agreement between warring groups to stop fighting. This agreement is sometimes made while the different sides try to reach a peace settlement.

chemical weapon A weapon that releases gases or poisons into the air which are harmful to humans.

civilian Someone who is not in the army.

Code of Conduct Guidelines for people to follow when there is a crisis.

drought A long period of time without rainfall.

economy The activities of a country which help it to earn money.

election A vote to decide the government of a country.

ethnic An ethnic group is a group of people who share the same race, nationality, culture or religion.

Gulf War The war in 1990–91 between the United States and its allies and Iraq. The war began when Iraq invaded Kuwait.

hostage A person who is held prisoner by a warring side, so that it can achieve certain aims, such as release of its prisoners.

human rights Rights that belong to everyone, such as the right to freedom of movement, shelter and education.

independent Free from rule by another country.

invade To send a force into another country with the aim of taking over that country.

irrigation Supplying land with water along canals or ditches to improve crop growth.

land mine An explosive weapon that is placed in the ground and is usually set off by someone stepping on it.

massacre The killing of large numbers of people.

Médecins Sans Frontières (MSF) An aid agency which offers medical help in a crisis. The name is French for 'doctors without borders'.

minority group A group that is racially different from the majority of people in a country.

persecution This describes when people are treated badly because of their race or religion.

pest A creature, such as a locust, that damages crops.

prisoner of war A soldier who is captured and held prisoner by the enemy.

racism The belief that some races of people are better than others. People may treat other races badly if they believe this.

Red Crescent A Muslim aid agency that is part of the Red Cross movement. Its symbol is a red crescent.

repatriation The sending back of people to their own country.

republic A country that has an elected person as its head, such as a president, rather than a king or queen.

revenge Harming someone because they have harmed you in the past.

sanction Action taken against a country because it has threatened world peace or ignored human rights. The idea is to punish the country to force it to change its policies.

self-sufficient Needing no help or support from anyone else.

Soviet Union A large communist country in Eastern Europe and Asia, formed of many different states. The Soviet Union split apart in 1991.

United Nations (UN) An organization of countries around the world which encourages world peace and offers help to people in a crisis.

Universal Declaration of Human Rights Part of international law that includes laws to protect the rights of refugees.

uprising The act of rebelling against a government or those in power.

INDEX

First published in Great Britain in 1998 by

Belitha Press Limited,
London House, Great Eastern Wharf
Parkgate Road, London SW11 4NQ

Copyright in this format © Belitha Press Limited 1998
Text copyright © Paul Bennett 1998

Series editor Julie Hill
Series designer Simeen Karim
Consultants Dr Peter Walker and Elizabeth Bassant
Picture researcher Diana Morris

ISBN 1 85561 793 5

British Library Cataloguing in Publication Data for this book is available from the British Library

Printed in Hong Kong

Photographic credits

Martin Adler/ Panos Pictures: 13t. James Baker/ Sipa/ Rex Features: 8b. Denis Cameron/ Rex Features: 16t. Juliet Coombe/ Rex: 26b. Neil Cooper/ Panos: 15b. DRC/ M. Szabo 12. Peter Fryer/ Panos Pictures: 29b. L.Gilbert/ Sygma: front cover, 10b, 28b. Ron Giling/ Still Pictures: 26t. Mike Goldwater/ Network: 9b. Teit Hornbak/ Still Pictures: 11t. ICRC: 2, contents, 8t, 14b, 18b, 19t, 22b / Eric Bouvet: 13b /David Chancellor: 24b, 25b/ © Daily Mirror: 25t/ P.Dutoit: 10t, 24t / Ligue: 17t / Till Mayer: 28t/ F. von Sury: 17b. Fiona McDougall/ Camera Press: 11b. MSF/ Gamma/ Noel Quidu: 7b. Antonello Nusca/ Gamma/ Frank Spooner Pictures: 20b. Helene Rogers/ Trip: 15t. Sipa/ RexFeatures: 19b. Jon Spaull/ Panos Pictures: 27b & 29t. Renaut Thomas/ Gamma/ Frank Spooner: 16b. GaryTrotter/ Still Pictures: 4. UNHCR: 9t, 22t / E.Brussard: 6t / A.Hollman: 20t, 21t, 21b / Y.Saita: 23b/ L.Taylor: 6b / J.Zaprzala: 23t. UNICEF: back cover & 18t, 30/ Lemoyne: title page & 7t /G.Pirozzi: 27t.

With thanks to the following for help with case study material: British Red Cross pp15, 25; ICRC p19; MSF p11; and UNHCR pp 7, 13, 21, 23, 29.